The Wonderful Towers of Watts

The Wonderful Towers of Watts

Patricia Zelver • pictures by Frané Lessac

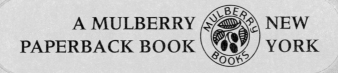

A MULBERRY PAPERBACK BOOK   MULBERRY BOOKS   NEW YORK

The Library of Congress has cataloged the Tambourine Books edition of
The Wonderful Towers of Watts as follows: Zelver, Patricia. The wonderful towers of
Watts/by Patricia Zelver; illustrated by Frané Lessac.—1st ed. p. cm.
Summary: Describes how an Italian immigrant built three unusual towers
in his backyard in the Watts neighborhood of Los Angeles.
ISBN 0-688-12649-9.—ISBN 0-688-12650-2 (LE)
1. Simon Rodia's Towers (Watts, Los Angeles, Calif.)—Juvenile literature. 2. Los
Angeles (Calif.)—Buildings, structures, etc.—Juvenile literature. [1. Simon
Rodia's Towers (Watts, Los Angeles, Calif.) 2. Los Angeles (Calif.)
—Buildings, structures, etc.] I. Lessac, Frané, ill. II. Title.
NA2930.Z46 1994 725'.97'092—dc20 93-20344 CIP AC

1 3 5 7 9 10 8 6 4 2
First Mulberry Edition, 1996
ISBN 0-688-14653-8

For Sam and Will and Bud Goldstone
P.Z.

For the children of Watts
F.L.

A lot of people thought Old Sam was crazy.

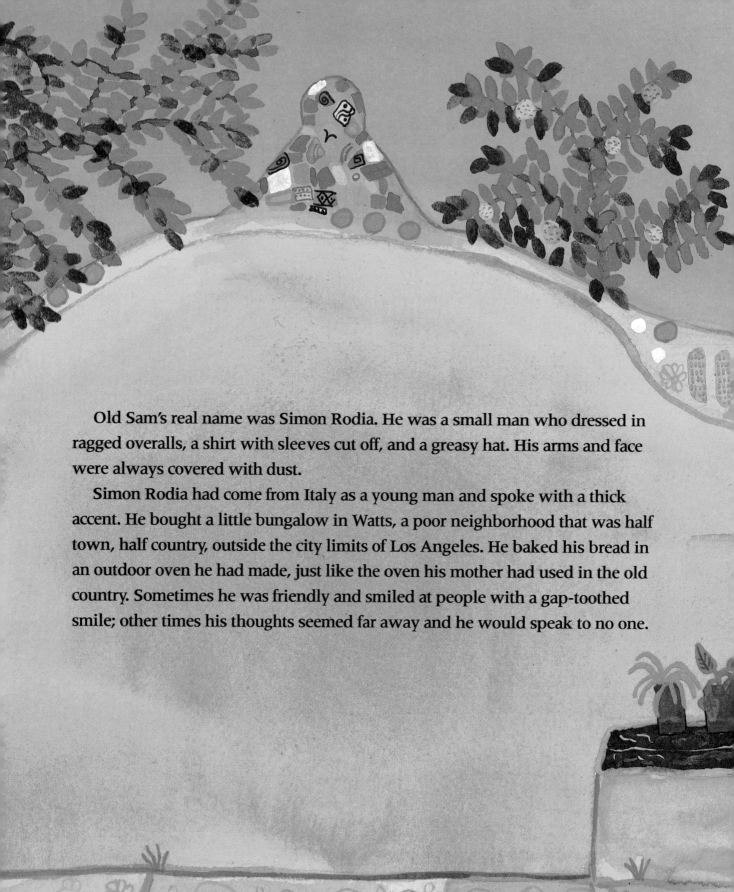

Old Sam's real name was Simon Rodia. He was a small man who dressed in ragged overalls, a shirt with sleeves cut off, and a greasy hat. His arms and face were always covered with dust.

Simon Rodia had come from Italy as a young man and spoke with a thick accent. He bought a little bungalow in Watts, a poor neighborhood that was half town, half country, outside the city limits of Los Angeles. He baked his bread in an outdoor oven he had made, just like the oven his mother had used in the old country. Sometimes he was friendly and smiled at people with a gap-toothed smile; other times his thoughts seemed far away and he would speak to no one.

Old Sam worked as a laborer at Taylor's Tilery. Every evening he got off the streetcar carrying a large burlap sack of broken colored tiles.

"What's Old Sam going to do with those?" people said.

On weekends Old Sam walked down to the vacant lot by the railroad tracks and collected things that people thought were better thrown away. He brought home blue Milk of Magnesia bottles, broken bits of colored pottery, even pieces of broken mirrors. Sometimes he paid the neighborhood kids pennies or cookies to bring him empty green soda pop bottles and sacks of seashells.

"What does Old Sam want with all that junk?" people wondered.

Old Sam spent most of his money on sacks of cement, sand, and steel.
People could hear him working in his backyard, behind a high fence.
    "Old Sam, what's he up to?" they said.

One day, to the neighbors' amazement, something strange and beautiful rose up over the fence in Sam's backyard. It was a lacy web of steel, covered with a skin of concrete in which Old Sam had stuck glittering bits of tile, glass, mirrors, pottery, and seashells. Was Old Sam building a fairy castle? A church spire? A tower on which he could climb to the sky?

Everyone stared in wonder at Old Sam's creation.

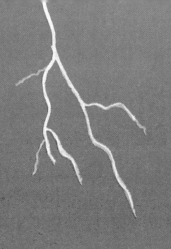

Sam went on working. He worked all by himself for thirty-three years in all kinds of weather, high off the ground with only a window washer's belt to keep him from falling. While he worked he listened to opera music on an old gramophone. His favorite singer was Enrico Caruso. Old Sam could be heard singing along with him.

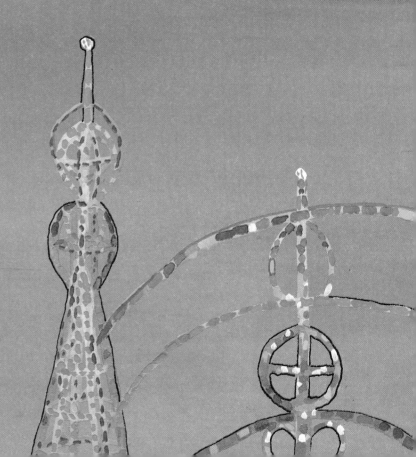

The children of the neighborhood grew up and had their own children, who watched Old Sam's towers soaring into the sky. Old Sam was getting older, too, but he went on working, just as before.

Sometimes Old Sam invited the neighborhood children into his yard, which was now surrounded by a decorated wall. Inside, the children found a magical city with little streets, squares, and fountains. The walks and walls were covered with starfish patterns, heart shapes, seashells, colorful tiles decorated with peacocks, and a golden bumblebee. Stuck into the cement were all sorts of curious objects which Old Sam had collected over the years. A teapot spout. A cowboy boot. Faucet handles. Horseshoes. Even willowware plates.

Newspaper reporters heard about the towers and came to see them and to talk to Old Sam.

"What do they mean?" they asked him.

Old Sam just smiled.

"Where are your plans?" they said.

Old Sam pointed to his head.

"Why did you do it?" they said.

"I just felt like it." Old Sam said.

One day when Sam was eighty years old, he gave the key to his house to a neighbor and went off to live near his relatives in another city. It was the last time he saw the towers. He never came back again.

Los Angeles grew up around Watts. The city officials decided the towers must be dangerous. They could fall down in an earthquake or in a windstorm. After all, they said, Old Sam was not an engineer. When some people who loved the towers heard this, they volunteered to make a wind-load test to prove the towers were safe. The towers passed the test and were saved.

Watts is still a poor part of Los Angeles. But no other place has the Watts Towers. Every year people come from all over the world to marvel at Old Sam's crazy dream.

ABOUT THE AUTHOR

Patricia Zelver's first book for Tambourine was *The Wedding of Don Octavio*, and she is also the author of two adult novels and a short story collection. Her stories have been selected eight times for *Prize Stories: The O. Henry Awards* and appeared in numerous other anthologies. She grew up in Medford, Oregon, and lives with her husband in California; they have two sons and two grandsons.

ABOUT THE ARTIST

Frané Lessac has illustrated several books for Tambourine, including her own *Caribbean Alphabet* and Jan Wahl's *Little Gray One*. A starred review of Irving Burgie's *Caribbean Carnival* in *Publishers Weekly* cited her "dynamic gouache paintings." Ms. Lessac was born in the United States; she currently lives in Australia with her husband and their two children.